COTE D'IVOIRE 2016 HUMAN RIGHTS REPORT

EXECUTIVE SUMMARY

Cote d'Ivoire is a democratic republic ruled by a freely elected government. In legislative elections held on December 18, the ruling government coalition won 66 percent of National Assembly seats. The main opposition party, which boycotted the 2011 legislative elections, participated and won seats. The elections were peaceful and considered inclusive and transparent. The country held a presidential election in October 2015, in which President Alassane Ouattara was re-elected by a significant majority. International and domestic observers judged the election to be free and fair.

Civilian authorities failed at times to maintain effective control over the security forces.

In April the United Nations lifted all sanctions on the country and renewed the mandate of the UN Operation in Cote d'Ivoire (UNOCI) for a final year, until June 2017. Despite continued but slow improvements in security and political reconciliation, the government's efforts to restore the rule of law and address impunity after the 2010-11 postelectoral crisis remained incomplete.

The most serious human rights problems were security force abuses, including extrajudicial killings and the abuse of detainees and prisoners, and the government's inability to enforce the rule of law. The Armed Forces of Cote d'Ivoire (FACI), formerly known as the Republican Forces of Cote d'Ivoire, and the gendarmerie were responsible for arbitrary arrests and detentions, including at the informal detention centers they operated.

Prison and detention center conditions were harsh and sometimes life threatening, and lengthy pretrial detention was a problem. The judiciary was inefficient and lacked independence. The government restricted freedom of press and assembly. Corruption in government was pervasive. Internally displaced persons (IDPs) faced insecure and difficult living conditions. Statelessness remained extensive. Discrimination, sexual assault, and violence against women and children occurred. Societal discrimination against ethnic groups, persons with disabilities, the lesbian, gay, bisexual, transgender, and intersex (LGBTI) community, and victims of HIV/AIDS were problems. Employers subjected children and informal-sector workers to forced labor and hazardous conditions, particularly in rural areas.

The government seldom took steps to prosecute officials who committed abuses, whether in the security services or elsewhere in the government, and impunity was a serious problem. Several high-level individuals aligned with the government were reportedly responsible for human rights violations in the 2010-11 postelectoral crisis, and some of those individuals retained senior security force positions.

There were allegations of sexual exploitation and abuse committed by UN peacekeepers deployed to UNOCI.

Section 1. Respect for the Integrity of the Person, Including Freedom from:

a. Arbitrary Deprivation of Life and other Unlawful or Politically Motivated Killings

There were several reports the government or its agents committed arbitrary or unlawful killings.

For example, on March 6, FACI soldiers used live ammunition to quell a demonstration in Assuefry, near Bondoukou; three protesters were killed and one injured. The demonstrators were protesting extortion by soldiers. The government made no arrests.

A terrorist attack resulted in civilian deaths. On March 13, a terrorist attack on a beach resort in Grand-Bassam resulted in the deaths of 16 civilians, including a child. The government arrested two soldiers and sentenced them to 10 years in prison for providing support to the terrorists in the preparation for the attack.

On January 28, the trial of former president, Laurent Gbagbo, and his close ally, Charles Ble Goude, opened at the International Criminal Court (ICC) in The Hague. Gbagbo and Ble Goude were accused of four counts each of crimes against humanity committed during the 2010-11 postelectoral crisis, in which at least 3,000 civilians were killed and more than 150 women and girls were raped.

On March 31, the trial of former first lady Simone Gbagbo commenced in the Assize Court for crimes against humanity and war crimes. (Simone Gbagbo, who has been in custody since 2011, also has been indicted by the ICC.) Hers was the first-ever trial for crimes against humanity conducted within the country. Some human rights groups acting as plaintiffs in the case withdrew during the year, claiming proceedings were flawed. Earlier in March the Supreme Court rejected

Simone Gbagbo's final appeal against the 20-year sentence resulting from a separate 2015 trial in which she was charged with crimes against the state.

On January 25, the trial of 19 military officers charged in connection with the 2002 assassination of General Robert Guei and his family resumed. On February 18, the military court sentenced three officers--General Dogbo Ble, former head of the Republican Guard; Commander Anselme Seka Yapo, former head of the protection detail for the former first lady; and Daleba Sery--to life imprisonment for murder and complicity in murder, and four others to 10 years' imprisonment. The remaining 12 were acquitted.

b. Disappearance

Unlike in the previous year, there were no reports of politically motivated disappearances.

c. Torture and Other Cruel, Inhuman, or Degrading Treatment or Punishment

The constitution and law prohibit such practices, but there were reports that government officials employed them.

According to a July report by UNOCI's Human Rights Division, there were 1,129 reported rape cases with 1,149 victims from 2012-15. Of that number, 76 percent of victims were children, and 7 percent of alleged perpetrators were state agents, particularly members of FACI and teachers.

According to Amnesty International, police raped one student and sexually abused another during university protests in April. The government denied the allegations and did not take action against the accused.

The United Nations reported that between January 1 and December 20, it received four allegations of sexual exploitation and abuse by UN peacekeepers deployed to UNOCI, with two alleged incidents occurring during the year, one in 2012, and one for which the date was unknown. These allegations involved military peacekeepers from Senegal, Niger, and Pakistan. Of the four allegations, two involved minors. The two allegations against Senegalese peacekeepers, one of which involved a minor, and the allegation against a Nigerien military observer, were being investigated by the United Nations. There was no result by the end of the year. The allegation against the Pakistani peacekeeper, which involved a minor, was being investigated by the government of Pakistan. There were no results by the end of the year.

Prison and Detention Center Conditions

Prison conditions were harsh and sometimes life threatening due to food shortages, gross overcrowding, inadequate sanitary conditions, and lack of medical care.

Physical Conditions: Overcrowding continued in many prisons. At the end of November, there were 11,192 prisoners, of whom an estimated 193 were minors and 237 were women. The central prison of Abidjan was built to hold approximately 1,500 prisoners but held 3,845 as of September 21. Reports from other prisons also indicated the number of inmates exceeded capacity.

Large prisons generally had doctors, while smaller prisons had nurses. Prisoners with health crises were supposed to be sent to health centers with doctors; however, critical health care for prisoners was not always available at local hospitals or clinics. Charities or religious organizations sometimes financed prisoners' medical care.

The International Committee of the Red Cross (ICRC) provided nutritional supplements to vulnerable prisoners, such as pregnant women and the elderly. Poor ventilation and high temperatures, exacerbated by overcrowding, were problems in some prisons.

According to government figures, 55 prisoners died through September 26. In February an armed confrontation between security forces and detainees at the central prison of Abidjan resulted in the deaths of a prison warden and 10 detainees, including Yacouba Coulibaly, alias "Yacou the Chinese," who, with his men, had reportedly controlled parts of the prison. Two trials resulting from the confrontation continued at year's end.

Authorities did not always hold men and women in separate prison wings, held juveniles with adults in the same cells in some prisons, and held pretrial detainees with convicted prisoners. The children of female inmates often lived with their mothers in prison, although prisons accepted no responsibility for their care or feeding. Inmate mothers received help from local and international nongovernmental organizations (NGOs).

Wealthy prisoners reportedly could buy extra cell space, food, and other amenities as well as hire staff to wash and iron their clothes. The government allotted 500 CFA francs ($0.85) per person per day for food rations, which was insufficient. Families routinely supplemented rations if they lived within proximity of the prison or detention center.

No information on conditions at irregular or informal detention centers operated by the FACI or Directorate for Territorial Surveillance (DST) was available, as the government did not allow local or international NGOs to access them.

Administration: Prison records were destroyed during the 2010-11 postelectoral crisis, and the government did not take significant measures to restore records. Record keeping that resumed after the crisis was not always adequate. The law provides for work-release programs and alternatives to incarceration for youths. In May, for example, 63 young offenders arrested in 2014 graduated from an 18-month reinsertion program in Bonoua, where they learned carpentry and sewing. Although sentencing magistrates were responsible for alternatives to sentencing and facilitating conditional release for inmates, there were fewer than 20 of them across all courts and they did not function effectively. There was no prison ombudsman, but prisoners could submit complaints to judicial authorities. Prison authorities had limited incentive or capacity to investigate and redress allegations of poor detention conditions. Prison administrators continued to detain or release prisoners outside normal legal procedures. There were reports of pretrial detainees receiving convictions in their absence due to lack of transport from prison to court.

Authorities generally permitted visitors in formal prisons. Prisoners' access to lawyers and families was allegedly intermittent or nonexistent in informal detention centers operated by the FACI and DST.

Independent Monitoring: The government generally permitted the United Nations and international NGOs adequate access to formal prisons. The government did not grant them access to informal detention centers run by the FACI and DST. Local human rights groups reported sporadic access to prisons.

Improvements: Unlike in the previous year, potable water was available in all formal prisons and detention centers, both for drinking and bathing.

d. Arbitrary Arrest or Detention

The constitution and law prohibit arbitrary arrest and detention, but both occurred. The FACI (which lacks arrest authority), DST, and other authorities arbitrarily arrested and detained persons, often without charge. They held many of these detainees briefly before releasing them or transferring them to formal prisons and detention centers, but detained others for lengthy periods. The United Nations reported several incidents of detention in undisclosed and unauthorized facilities.

Role of the Police and Security Apparatus

Police (under the Ministry of Interior and Security) and gendarmerie (under the Ministry of Defense) are responsible for law enforcement. The Coordination Center for Operational Decisions (CCDO), a mixed unit of police, gendarmerie, and FACI personnel, assisted police in providing security in some large cities. The FACI (under the Ministry of Defense) is responsible for national defense. The DST (under the Ministry of Interior and Security) has responsibility for countering external threats. The FACI, who were better trained and equipped than police or gendarmerie, continued to perform functions normally associated with those entities. The national gendarmerie assumed control from the FACI for all security functions on national roadways, such as running authorized checkpoints. Nevertheless, the FACI still operated unauthorized security checkpoints, especially near borders, where they engaged in extortion.

While FACI forces were better trained and equipped than police or gendarmes, they were not adequately trained or equipped and lacked an adequate command and control structure. Corruption and impunity were endemic in the FACI and other security forces, including police, gendarmerie, CCDO, and DST.

Dozos (traditional hunters) assumed an informal security role in many communities, although they had no legal authority to arrest or detain. The government discouraged the Dozos, whom most residents feared, from assuming security roles.

Military police and the military tribunal are responsible for investigating and prosecuting alleged internal abuses perpetrated by the security services, but investigations and prosecutions rarely occurred.

Security forces failed at times to prevent or respond to societal violence, particularly during intercommunal clashes over land tenure. In some cases gendarmes or FACI personnel restored order when police failed to respond.

On March 2, in collaboration with the Economic Community of West African States, the government adopted a decree establishing a national center to coordinate early warning responses to crises. The role of the center, which was not operational by year's end, included preventing conflict, fighting terrorism, and reducing response times following crisis alerts.

In June the Cell for Coordination and Monitoring of Reintegration (CCSR)--created in July 2015 to continue the reintegration process for ex-combatants following the expiration of the mandate of the Authority for Disarmament, Demobilization, and Reintegration (ADDR)--completed its work. According to the government, more than 69,000 former combatants were reintegrated as a result of ADDR and CCSR processes.

Arrest Procedures and Treatment of Detainees

The law allows investigative magistrates or the national prosecutor to order the detention of a suspect for 48 hours without bringing charges. Nevertheless, police often arrested individuals and held them without charge beyond the legal limit. In special cases, such as suspected actions against state security, the national prosecutor can authorize an additional 48-hour period of preventive custody. An investigating magistrate can request pretrial detention for up to four months at a time by submitting a written justification to the national prosecutor. First-time offenders charged with minor offenses may be held for a maximum of five days after their initial hearing before the investigative magistrate. Repeat minor offenders and those accused of felonies may be held for six and 18 months, respectively.

While the law provides for informing detainees promptly of the charges against them, this did not always occur, especially in cases concerning state security and involving the FACI and the DST. In other cases magistrates could not verify whether detainees who were not charged had been released. A bail system exists but was used solely at the discretion of the trial judge. Authorities generally allowed detainees to have access to lawyers. In cases involving national security, authorities did not allow access to lawyers and family members. For other serious crimes, the government provided lawyers to those who could not afford them, but offenders charged with less serious offenses often had no lawyer. Human rights observers reported multiple instances in which detainees were transferred to detention facilities outside of their presiding judge's jurisdiction, in violation of the law.

<u>Arbitrary Arrest</u>: On August 10, DST agents arrested without warrant Antoinette Meho, leader of the women's wing of the opposition Ivoirian Popular Front (FPI). Meho was held without access to family or her lawyers for several days before being transferred to the central prison in Abidjan. According to the justice minister, Meho was charged with undermining state security and remained in detention awaiting trial at year's end.

<u>Pretrial Detention</u>: Prolonged pretrial detention was a problem. According to government figures, as of September 21, approximately 44 percent of all prison inmates and 57 percent of inmates at Abidjan's central prison were in pretrial detention, including some minors. In many cases the length of detention equaled or exceeded the sentence for the alleged crime. Inadequate staffing in the judicial ministry, judicial inefficiency, and lack of training contributed to lengthy pretrial detention.

<u>Detainee's Ability to Challenge Lawfulness of Detention before a Court</u>: Although detainees have the right to challenge in court the lawfulness of their detention and to obtain release if found to have been unlawfully detained, this rarely occurred because most detainees were unaware of this right and had limited access to public defenders.

e. Denial of Fair Public Trial

The constitution and law provide for an independent judiciary, and the judiciary generally was independent in ordinary criminal cases. The judiciary was inadequately resourced and inefficient. The continued lack of civilian indictments against pro-Ouattara elements for crimes during the 2010-11 postelectoral crisis indicated the judiciary was subject to political and executive influence. There were also numerous reports of judicial corruption, and bribes often influenced rulings. During the last two years, the General Inspectorate of Judicial Inspections opened disciplinary investigations based on field audits of all 36 courts in the country; however, no magistrates or clerks had been disciplined or dismissed by year's end.

Trial Procedures

The constitution and law provide for the right to a fair public trial, but the judiciary did not enforce this right. Although the law provides for the presumption of innocence and the right to be informed promptly and in detail of the charges (with free interpretation as necessary from the moment charged through all appeals), the government did not always respect this requirement. In the past Assize Courts (special courts convened as needed to try criminal cases involving major crimes) rarely convened. Starting in 2015, however, they convened for one session per year in several cities to hear a backlog of cases. Defendants accused of felonies have the right to legal counsel at their own expense. Other defendants may also seek legal counsel. The judicial system provides for court-appointed attorneys, although only limited free legal assistance was available; the government had a small legal defense fund to pay members of the bar who agreed to represent the indigent. Defendants have the right to adequate time and facilities to prepare a defense. Defendants may not access government-held evidence, although their attorneys have the legal right to do so. Defendants may present their own witnesses or evidence and confront prosecution or plaintiff witnesses. Lack of a witness protection mechanism was a problem. Defendants cannot be legally compelled to testify or confess guilt, although there were reports this abuse sometimes occurred. Defendants have the right to be present at their trials, but courts may try defendants in their absence. Those convicted had access to appeals courts in Abidjan, Bouake, and Daloa, but higher courts rarely overturned verdicts.

Military tribunals did not try civilians or provide the same rights as civilian criminal courts. Although there are no appellate courts within the military court system, persons convicted by a military tribunal may petition the Supreme Court to order a retrial.

The relative scarcity of trained magistrates and lawyers resulted in limited access to effective judicial proceedings, particularly outside of major cities. In rural areas traditional institutions often administered justice at the village level, handling domestic disputes and minor land questions in accordance with customary law. Dispute resolution was by extended debate. There were no reported instances of physical punishment. The law specifically provides for a "grand mediator," appointed by the president, to bridge traditional and modern methods of dispute resolution.

Political Prisoners and Detainees

Amnesty International listed 226 persons arrested between the beginning of 2011 and September as political prisoners. Of the 226, all of whom remained in prison at year's end, 20 suffered from various ailments, and more than half were malnourished.

Some political parties and local human rights groups claimed members of former president Gbagbo's FPI party--detained on charges, including economic crimes, armed robbery, looting, and embezzlement--were political prisoners, especially when charged for actions committed during the 2010-11 postelectoral crisis.

Opposition and government representatives offered differing assessments of the number of political detainees remaining in custody. A government-created platform for dialogue with the opposition met several times during the year to discuss these detainees and other issues concerning the opposition. The government released all but three of the 90 persons arrested in connection with the 2015 presidential election. In September the government released 10 persons associated with the FPI, and in March it released 70 of 300 persons whose release was requested by the FPI.

Political prisoners were given the same protections as other prisoners, including ICRC access.

Civil Judicial Procedures and Remedies

The constitution and law provide for an independent judiciary in civil matters, but the judiciary was subject to corruption, outside influence, and favoritism based on family and ethnic ties. Citizens may bring lawsuits seeking damages for, or cessation of, a human rights violation, but they did so infrequently. Individuals and organizations may appeal adverse domestic decisions to regional human rights bodies. The judiciary was slow and inefficient, and there were problems in enforcing domestic court orders.

f. Arbitrary or Unlawful Interference with Privacy, Family, Home, or Correspondence

The constitution and law prohibit such actions, but the government did not always respect these prohibitions. The law requires warrants for security personnel to conduct searches, the prosecutor's agreement to retain any evidence seized in a search, and the presence of witnesses in a search, which may take place at any time. Police sometimes used a general search warrant without a name or address. The FACI and DST arrested individuals without warrants.

In some areas FACI units continued to occupy illegally businesses and homes, despite the government's efforts to end such occupations.

Some leaders of opposition parties reported authorities froze their bank accounts, although they were not on any international sanctions list, and courts had not charged them with any offenses.

A government-opposition dialogue platform discussed occupied housing and frozen bank accounts, with some progress acknowledged by representatives from both sides. In March the government stated 43 bank accounts remained frozen after it reactivated four bank accounts belonging to associates of former president Gbagbo. In August the government reactivated 12 more bank accounts of FPI officials.

Section 2. Respect for Civil Liberties, Including:

a. Freedom of Speech and Press

The constitution and law provide for freedom of speech and press, but the government restricted both. The National Press Council (CNP), the government's print media regulatory body, briefly suspended or reprimanded newspapers and journalists for statements it contended were false, libelous, or perceived to incite xenophobia and hate.

<u>Freedom of Speech and Expression</u>: The law prohibits incitement to violence, ethnic hatred, rebellion, and insulting the head of state or other senior members of the government.

In May the CNP suspended for one month a journalist with *LG Infos*, a pro-Gbagbo daily newspaper, who wrote an article about an alleged shooting that resulted in the death of a young French-Lebanese man in front of the president's residence. The CNP ruled that the information was false and led to xenophobic and hateful discourse.

<u>Press and Media Freedoms</u>: The independent media were active and expressed a wide variety of views. Newspapers aligned politically with the opposition frequently published inflammatory editorials against the government or fabricated stories to defame political opponents.

The High Audiovisual Communications Authority oversees the regulation and operation of radio and television stations. There were numerous independent radio stations. The law prohibits transmission of political commentary by private radio stations. There were no private television stations.

In a continuing effort at media liberalization, on March 1, the High Audiovisual Communications Authority announced the results of the 2015 bidding by private cable and satellite television providers for operating licenses. Three multinational companies received licenses, and the Ministry of Communication stated the companies would have complete editorial freedom and the option of transmitting locally produced content, such as news and other informational programs. An additional bidding process for local providers opened in May.

Censorship or Content Restrictions: The government influenced news coverage and program content on television channels and public and private radio stations. In February the state-run Ivoirian Radio and Television suspended production of live television and radio programs by some religious groups, NGOs, and traditional healers; the suspension remained in effect at year's end.

Libel/Slander Laws: Criminal libel is punishable by one to three years in prison.

National Security: Libel deemed to threaten the national interest is punishable by six months to five years in prison.

Internet Freedom

The government did not restrict or disrupt access to the internet or censor online content, and there were no credible reports that the government monitored private online communications without appropriate legal authority. Authorities permitted suspended newspapers to publish their full content online. One website estimated 22 percent of the population had home-based access to the internet via computer or mobile device. With a mobile phone penetration rate of virtually 100 percent, however, internet access by mobile device was likely much higher.

Academic Freedom and Cultural Events

There were no government restrictions on academic freedom or cultural events. Violent clashes in July, however, between security forces and student unions protesting the government's plan to house athletes in the Francophone Games in student housing at the University of Felix Houphouet-Boigny in Abidjan during the summer of 2017 resulted in injuries to students and security force members. Approximately 30 students were arrested. The government subsequently suspended all student union activities on university grounds and stationed security forces at the university.

b. Freedom of Peaceful Assembly and Association

Freedom of Assembly

The law provides for freedom of assembly, but the government did not always respect this right. The law requires groups that wish to hold demonstrations or rallies in stadiums or other enclosed spaces to submit a written notice to the Ministry of Interior three days before the proposed event. Numerous opposition political groups reported denials of their requests to hold political meetings and alleged inconsistent standards for granting public assembly permissions. In some instances public officials stated they could not provide for the safety of opposition groups attempting to organize both public and private meetings.

In July, in Yopougon (a Gbagbo-leaning neighborhood in western Abidjan), police arrested three pro-Gbagbo activists organizing the signing of a petition for the release of the former president from the ICC. They were released after two weeks.

Police use of excessive force to disperse demonstrators resulted in injuries and at least one death. In August the military tribunal sentenced Staff Sergeant Gervais Zoukou to 18 months in prison for striking a student with disabilities with his car during June protests at the University of Felix Houphouet-Boigny. The student subsequently died.

Freedom of Association

The law provides for freedom of association, and the government generally respected this right. While the law prohibits the formation of political parties along ethnic or religious lines, ethnicity was often a key factor in party membership.

c. Freedom of Religion

See the Department of State's *International Religious Freedom Report* at www.state.gov/religiousfreedomreport/.

d. Freedom of Movement, Internally Displaced Persons, Protection of Refugees, and Stateless Persons

The constitution and law do not specifically provide for freedom of movement, foreign travel, emigration, or repatriation, but the government generally respected these rights. The government cooperated with the Office of the UN High Commissioner for Refugees (UNHCR) and other humanitarian organizations in providing protection and assistance to internally displaced persons, refugees, returning refugees, asylum seekers, stateless persons, or other persons of concern.

In-country Movement: There were impediments to internal travel. Security forces and unidentified groups erected and operated roadblocks, primarily along secondary roads outside of Abidjan. Although some roadblocks served legitimate security purposes, racketeering and extortion were common. For example, FACI engaged in racketeering at illegal checkpoints with the participation of gendarmes and police. By the end of September, a police antiracketeering task force working with the High Authority for Good Governance (HABG) identified 59 cases for prosecution. Two of the accused were convicted of racketeering by year's end.

Exile: Several loyalists to former president Gbagbo, some with pending criminal charges, remained in self-imposed exile.

Emigration and Repatriation: Of the more than 39,000 Ivoirian refugees who remained outside the country, more than 19,000 were in Liberia. Due to concerns over the possible spread of ebola, the borders with Liberia and Guinea officially remained closed until September. Nevertheless, in December 2015 humanitarian corridors to resume voluntary repatriation of refugees from Liberia were opened, despite the closure of the border for all other travelers. From January through September, UNHCR assisted the return of more than 18,000 refugees, primarily from Liberia. With the opening of the border with Guinea in September, UNHCR facilitated the repatriation of an additional 128 refugees from Guinea.

Internally Displaced Persons

Most IDPs were in the western and northeastern regions and in Abidjan and surrounding suburbs; no estimates of the total number of IDPs were available. Most IDPs were displaced due to the 2010-11 postelectoral crisis and evictions from illegally occupied protected forests. For example, the United Nations estimated more than 51,000 persons were evicted during the summer from Mont Peko National Park, where they were living and farming illegally. Unlike in the previous year, there were no reports the government evicted residents of Abidjan from flood-prone areas or removed structures built on illegally occupied land.

In 2014 the government adopted the African Union Convention for the Protection and Assistance of Internally Displaced Persons in Africa (Kampala Convention). The convention commits the government to protect the rights and well-being of persons displaced by conflict, violence, disasters, or human rights abuses and provides a framework of durable solutions for IDPs. The government respected the principle of voluntary return but provided limited assistance to IDPs; the United Nations and international and local NGOs worked to fill the gaps. While many of those displaced returned to their areas of origin, difficult conditions, including lack of access to land, shelter, and security, prevented others' return. Host communities had few resources to receive and assist IDPs, who often resorted to living in informal urban settlements.

Protection of Refugees

Access to Asylum: The constitution and law provide for the granting of asylum or refugee status, and the government has established a system for providing protection to refugees. According to UNHCR the country hosted fewer than 1,400 refugees, most of whom were Liberian refugees who opted for local integration following the 2012 invocation of the cessation clause, which ended refugee status for Liberians. All 103 Liberian refugees who applied for formal resettlement in the country were accepted and remained in the country.

Durable Solutions: The government facilitated local integration for refugees in the most extreme situations by issuing resident permits to all refugees more than 14 years old to allow them to move freely in the country. Refugees also had access to naturalization, although UNHCR reported many had been in the naturalization process for more than five years.

Temporary Protection: The government also provided temporary protection for individuals who no longer qualified as refugees under the relevant UN conventions. Persons awaiting status determination received a letter, valid for three months, indicating they were awaiting a decision on their status. The letter provided for temporary stay and freedom of movement only. Holders of the letter did not qualify for refugee assistance such as access to education or health care.

Stateless Persons

Statelessness in the country remained extensive. Citizenship is derived from one's parents rather than by birth within the country's territory, and birth registration was not universal. The country had habitual residents who were either legally stateless or effectively stateless. UNHCR continued to estimate the number of stateless persons at 700,000.

The special declaration program--based on a 2013 law that allows foreign-born persons living in the country before independence in 1960 to obtain citizenship by declaration and gives foreign nationals born in the country between 1961 and 1973 the option of citizenship--ended on January 24. Casework continued on the 123,810 claims submitted, and approximately 12,000 claimants received administrative nationality certificates. Responsibility for the final step--converting the nationality certificate into the ultimate proof of nationality (a judicial nationality certificate)--was on the claimant.

The National Action Plan to eradicate statelessness in the country was completed in Grand Bassam during a September 8-9 workshop organized by the Ministry of Justice. The plan delineates the steps required to uphold the government's obligations under statelessness conventions, including legal reform to provide for access to nationality for stateless persons not included in the declaration program (other historic migrants, foundlings, and others).

Section 3. Freedom to Participate in the Political Process

The constitution and law provide citizens the ability to choose their government in free and fair periodic elections held by secret ballot and based on universal and equal suffrage.

Elections and Political Participation

Recent Elections: In legislative elections held on December 18, the ruling government coalition won 66 percent of the 255 National Assembly seats. The main opposition party, which boycotted the 2011 legislative elections, participated and won seats. The elections were considered peaceful, inclusive, and transparent. In the October 2015 presidential election, President Alassane Ouattara was re-elected by a significant majority. International and domestic observers judged this election to be free and fair.

On October 30, the government conducted a referendum on a new constitution to replace the postmilitary coup constitution of 2000. The process for drafting the new constitution--and to a certain extent the content itself--was contentious. Opposition parties and some local and international organizations claimed the process was neither inclusive nor transparent and criticized the new text for strengthening the role of the executive branch. Despite an opposition boycott, the referendum passed overwhelmingly in a peaceful process that was inclusive and generally transparent.

Political Parties and Political Participation: The law prohibits the formation of political parties along ethnic or religious lines. Ethnicity, however, was often a key factor in party membership. Opposition leaders reported denials of their requests to hold political meetings and alleged inconsistent standards for granting public assembly permits.

For example, on October 3, the prefect of the district of Abidjan refused a permit for the planned October 5 opposition sit-in at the national assembly, where the president was scheduled to present the new constitution to deputies. The opposition postponed its protest until the following Saturday, but opposition leader, Mamadou Koulibaly, defied the ban and was arrested; Koulibaly was released two hours later.

Participation of Women and Minorities: There are no laws limiting the participation of women and members of minorities in the political process, and women and minorities did so. Cultural and traditional beliefs, however, limited the role of women. Of 253 national assembly members, 26 were women; of 197 mayors, 11 were women; of 31 regional council presidents, one was a woman. A few women held more prominent positions, including that of first vice president of the national assembly, nine of 36 cabinet ministers, and several chairs of important commissions.

Section 4. Corruption and Lack of Transparency in Government

The law provides criminal penalties for corruption by officials, but the government did not implement the law effectively, and officials frequently engaged in corrupt practices with impunity. Media and human rights groups reported significant official corruption. Transparency International indicated corruption was a severe problem, having the greatest effect on judicial proceedings, accountability of the security forces, contract awards, and customs and tax matters.

Corruption: On May 26, the government fired the director and deputy director of the Cotton and Cashew Council following an audit.

In May the High Authority for Good Governance, an independent administrative authority with legal and financial autonomy, reported corruption in 33 percent of the cases it investigated; 64 percent of HABG cases originated from public submissions.

The Independent National Public Procurement Regulatory Agency (ANRMP) is responsible for supporting, monitoring, and enforcing fair competition for government contracts. Following a 2014 report that 57 percent of all government contracts were sole-sourced, ANRMP began auditing government contracts. It found that from March 2015 to March, 78 percent of approved contracts were executed through competitive bidding.

Financial Disclosure: A presidential decree requires the head of state, ministers, heads of national institutions, and directors of administration to disclose their income and assets. Unlike in the past, when there was no penalty for noncompliance, in March 2015 the HABG started requiring public officials to submit a wealth declaration within 30 days of the beginning of their term in office. The declaration was confidential, but the list of those who have declared their wealth was publicly accessible in the official government journal. Officials who did not comply or provided a false declaration faced fines equal to six months of their salary. As of October approximately 50 percent of officials had declared their assets, and no one had been fined.

Public Access to Information: The law grants public access to government data, with the exception of information vital for the preservation of state security. Data relating to government activities and budgeting was largely available but varied among ministries and was often delayed. Much of the Ministry of Finance's data, including the national budget, was accessible on its website. Public procurement was generally transparent. The ANRMP quickly provided key information on procurement without charge, and it had a transparent decision making and public appeals process. If requested data was not provided, ANRMP referred the case to the Public Documents and Public Interest Information Access Commission, an independent administrative authority with the power to compel and sanction other public institutions not complying with the law.

Section 5. Governmental Attitude Regarding International and Nongovernmental Investigation of Alleged Violations of Human Rights

A number of international and domestic human rights groups generally operated without government restriction, investigating and publishing their findings on human rights cases. Government officials often were cooperative and responsive to their views.

<u>Government Human Rights Bodies</u>: In a January cabinet reshuffle, the president created the Ministry of Human Rights and Public Freedom, headed by Paulette Badjo Ezouehu, former head of the National Human Rights Commission (CNDH). The government-funded ministry is responsible for implementing and monitoring the government's policy on human rights, a function previously under the Ministry of Justice. The CNDH is an advisory body under the Ministry of Human Rights and consults on, conducts evaluations of, and creates proposals to promote, protect, and defend human rights. The ministry was neither adequately funded nor effective.

During the January cabinet reshuffle, the government also created the Ministry of Solidarity, Social Cohesion, and Victims' Compensation, funded by the government and headed by Mariatou Kone. Before creation of the ministry, issues of social cohesion and victim compensation were the responsibility of two state institutions--the National Commission for Reconciliation and Reparations for Victims in Cote d'Ivoire (CONARIV) and the National Program for Social Cohesion. During the year the ministry, which had an adequate budget and operated effectively, facilitated the voluntary repatriation of refugees, promoting social cohesion and compensating victims of crises based on a CONARIV list. The elevation of these issues to ministerial level reflected the president's stated second-term goal of reconciliation.

In January, UNOCI and the FACI added the CNDH to the Joint Mechanism on Human Rights to share information, address allegations of FACI human rights violations, and coordinate human rights activities within the FACI. In August the CNDH began opening offices outside Abidjan to assume some of the monitoring and other activities from UNOCI's Human Rights Division, which was scheduled to close in March 2017. Although the CNDH is chartered as a nongovernmental independent body, its funding was fully dependent on approval by the Ministry of Justice, and its offices outside of Abidjan were not fully staffed or equipped.

The civilian-controlled Special Investigative Cell (Special Cell) within the Ministry of Justice continued to investigate and try alleged perpetrators of human rights abuses committed during the postelectoral crisis. The Special Cell had an indefinite mandate but lacked sufficient resources and staff.

In March 2015 the government established CONARIV to provide for and distribute monetary compensation to victims of the crises from 1990 to 2011. The government allocated 10 billion CFA francs ($17,035,000) for this effort. On

April 19, CONARIV presented its final report to the president, including a consolidated list of victims, a draft reconciliation plan, and a national reparation policy proposal. CONARIV validated applications for compensation of 316,954 victims from the 874,056 requests submitted to it. CONARIV officially concluded its activities at the end of April, and the Ministry of Solidarity, Social Cohesion, and Victims' Compensation was responsible for paying reparations. CONARIV's final report and recommendations were not made public.

Section 6. Discrimination, Societal Abuses, and Trafficking in Persons

Women

<u>Rape and Domestic Violence</u>: The law prohibits rape and provides for prison terms of five to 20 years for perpetrators. The law does not specifically penalize spousal rape. A life sentence can be imposed in cases of gang rape if the rapists are related to or hold positions of authority over the victim, or if the victim is under 15 years of age. Most rape cases were tried on the lesser charge of "indecent assault," which carries a prison term of six months to five years. Of the 20 rape cases tried between October 2015 and June in four Assize Court sessions, 14 resulted in convictions with prison terms of between three and 10 years.

The government made some efforts to enforce the law, but local and international human rights groups reported rape remained widespread. UNOCI reported dozens of rape cases through September, including a number of gang rapes and rape by members of FACI (see section 1.c.). For these crimes civilian perpetrators either were convicted for crimes of lesser offense or were still in pretrial detention. Convicted perpetrators received between one month and 10 years' imprisonment.

Relatives, police, and traditional leaders often pressured female victims to seek an amicable resolution with the rapist rather than pursue a criminal case. In July the Ministry of Justice issued a circular advising that rape cases tried on a lesser charge violated the law and that amicable resolution of a case with the rapist should not stop investigation or the legal process.

Psychosocial services for rape victims were available with support from NGOs in some areas. Rape victims were no longer required to obtain a medical certificate, which could cost up to 50,000 CFA francs ($85) to move a legal complaint forward. As a practical matter, however, cases rarely proceeded without one since it often served as the primary form of evidence. In an August interministerial circular, the government announced gendarmes and police could no longer ask victims for a medical certificate and that a victim's complaint--whether written or verbal--was sufficient to initiate an investigation. Nevertheless, police lacked the training and equipment to investigate rape cases, so medical certificates often were the only evidence available.

The law does not specifically outlaw domestic violence, which was a serious and widespread problem. According to the Ministry for the Promotion of Women, Family, and Child Protection, more than 36 percent of women reported being victims of physical or psychological abuse at some time. Victims seldom reported domestic violence due to cultural barriers and because police often ignored women who reported rape or domestic violence. Many victims' families reportedly urged victims to withdraw complaints and remain with an abusive partner due to fear of social stigmatization.

In July the Ministry for the Promotion of Women, Family, and Child Protection approved the creation of a national program against gender-based violence, in coordination with the UN Action against Sexual Violence in Conflict. Key goals included preventing gender-based violence, coordinating a multisectoral response, and eliminating impunity.

The Ministry for the Promotion of Women, Family, and Child Protection assisted victims of domestic violence and rape, including counseling at government-operated centers. The National Committee to Fight Violence against Women and Children monitored abusive situations and made weekly radio announcements about hotlines for victims.

In June the government created the National Committee to Fight against Sexual Violence Related to Conflict under the authority of the president; in November the committee met in Grand Bassam. The chief of staff of the army, the minister of defense, and key sectoral ministries were charged with working together with the committee.

Female Genital Mutilation/Cutting (FGM/C): FGM/C was a serious problem. The predominant form of FGM/C was Type II--removal of clitoris and labia--although infibulation also occurred. The law specifically forbids FGM/C and provides penalties for practitioners of up to five years' imprisonment and fines of 360,000 to two million CFA francs ($610 to $3,400). Double penalties apply to medical practitioners. FGM/C was most common among rural populations in the northern regions, where approximately 70 percent of women and girls had been subjected to the practice, followed by the center-north part of the country (50 percent) and the

Abidjan region (36 percent). The procedure was generally performed before a girl reached age five. Local NGOs continued public awareness programs and worked to persuade practitioners to stop. The government successfully prosecuted some FGM/C cases during the year.

During a February event to mark the International Day of Zero Tolerance for Female Genital Mutilation, Euphrasie Kouassi Yao, the minister for the Promotion of Women, Family, and Child Protection, said the government was starting to pursue persons who ordered and assisted FGM/C through more effective implementation of the existing law. No further details were available.

Other Harmful Traditional Practices: Societal violence against women included traditional practices, such as dowry deaths (the killing of brides over dowry disputes), levirate (forcing a widow to marry her dead husband's brother), and sororate (forcing a woman to marry her dead sister's husband).

Sexual Harassment: The law prohibits sexual harassment and prescribes penalties of between one and three years' imprisonment and fines of 360,000 to one million CFA francs ($610 to $1,700). Nevertheless, the government rarely enforced the law, and harassment was widespread and routinely tolerated. In 2015 Anne-Desiree Ouloto, the then minister for the Promotion of Women, Family, and Child Protection, stated 38 percent of students experienced sexual harassment in school, and teachers sexually harassed 14 percent of students.

Reproductive Rights: Couples and individuals have the right to decide the number, spacing, and timing of their children; manage their reproductive health; and have access to the information and means to do so, free from coercion, discrimination, or violence. Government policy requires emergency health care services to be available and free to all, but care was not available in all regions, particularly rural areas, and was often expensive. Family planning indicators remained low, and the government's ability to deliver high quality maternal and reproductive health service was weak.

Only 14 percent of girls and women between ages 15 and 49 used a modern method of contraception. Unmet need for family planning was at 27 percent nationally and above 30 percent for the poorest women and girls. Thirty percent of adolescent girls had been or were pregnant when surveyed, a percentage that rose to 46 percent in rural areas. Threats or perceived threats of violence from husbands or other family members inhibited some women from seeking family planning or health services. In urban areas access to contraception and skilled attendance during childbirth were available to women who could afford them. According to the 2011-12 Demographic Health Survey, approximately 57.4 percent of pregnant women gave birth in a health facility. For women who were poor or lived in rural areas, transportation and the cost of services posed significant barriers to accessing health centers and hospitals.

According to the UN Population Fund, in 2015 the maternal mortality rate was 645 deaths per 100,000 live births; in 2010 the rate was 717 per 100,000. In addition to lack of access to adequate maternal health care services, factors contributing to the high maternal mortality rate included repeated pregnancies spaced too close together, each of which carried the risk of obstetric complications; incomplete abortions; the prevalence of HIV/AIDS; and FGM/C scarification, which often resulted in obstructed labor.

The penal code, which penalizes abortion in all cases unless the pregnancy puts the mother's life in danger, contributed to a high number of undesired pregnancies. Approximately two in five women had their first child before age 18, and approximately half of these births ended in poor outcomes as a result of unsuccessful attempts to seek illegal abortions performed by traditional healers or to abort by using medicinal plants, pills, broken bottles, or other sharp objects. Although women and girls who resorted to illicit abortions theoretically could access emergency health care, most were reluctant to do so since abortion was illegal.

Discrimination: The law provides for the same legal status and rights for women as for men in labor law but not under religious, personal status, property, nationality, and inheritance laws. Women experienced discrimination in marriage, divorce, child custody, employment, credit, pay, owning or managing businesses or property, education, the judicial process, and housing. In 2012 parliament passed a series of laws to reduce gender inequality in marriage, including laws to allow married women to benefit from an income tax deduction and to be involved in family decisions. Many religious and traditional authorities rejected these laws, however, and there was no evidence the government enforced them.

Some women had trouble obtaining loans because they could not meet lending criteria, including requirements for posting expensive household assets as collateral, which may not have a woman listed on the title. Women also experienced economic discrimination in owning or managing businesses.

Women's organizations continued to campaign for tax reform to enable single mothers to receive deductions for their children. Inheritance law also discriminates against women.

Women's advocacy organizations continued to sponsor campaigns against forced marriage, patterns of inheritance that excluded women, and other practices considered harmful to women and girls. They also campaigned against legal provisions that discriminated against women and continued their efforts to promote greater women's participation in national and local politics.

Children

Birth Registration: Citizenship is derived from one's parents. At least one parent must be a citizen for a child to acquire citizenship at birth. For births that occur outside health clinics, the law provides parents a three-month period to register their child's birth for a fee of 500 CFA francs ($0.85). According to some reports, the actual cost for birth registration was higher due to corrupt officials demanding bribes. For births that occurred in health clinics, the government charged no registration fee if parents submitted the appropriate documentation within 30 days of birth. More than two million children below 17 years old were not registered, including at least 1.5 million who were under age five. Although the government did not officially deny public services such as education or health care to children without documents, some schools reportedly required parents to present children's identity documents before enrolling them. Children without documents could not continue their studies after primary school.

Education: Education was free and compulsory for children ages six to 16. Parents of children not in compliance with the law are subjected to fines up to 500,000 CFA francs ($850) or jail time of two to six months. In principle students do not have to pay for books, uniforms, or fees, but some reportedly did because the government did not cover these expenses for every student. Some schools expected parents to contribute to the teachers' salaries and living stipends, particularly in rural areas. Students who failed secondary school entrance exams did not qualify for free public secondary education, and many families could not afford to pay for private schooling.

Educational participation of girls was lower than that of boys, particularly in rural areas. Parental preference for educating boys rather than girls reportedly persisted, particularly in rural areas. Most schools had inadequate sanitary facilities for girls. Rates of pregnancy among school girls were high. There were numerous reports of teachers demanding sexual favors from students in exchange for money or grades. Schools reported some girls did not return to school after vacation due to an early or forced marriage.

During the year the Ministry of Health and Public Hygiene, working with its financial and technical partners, implemented awareness programs to encourage children to stay in school. The ministry also worked with teachers to enable them to detect at early stages problems such as pregnancy, sexual exploitation, and violence.

Child Abuse: The penalty for statutory rape or attempted rape of a child under age 16 is a prison sentence of one to three years and a fine of 360,000 to one million CFA francs ($610 to $1,700). Nevertheless, children were victims of physical and sexual violence and abuse. Authorities reported rapes of girls as young as age five during the year. Authorities often reclassified claims of child rape as indecent assault since penalties were less severe. There were some prosecutions and convictions during the year. To assist child victims of violence and abuse, the government cooperated with the UN Children's Fund (UNICEF) to strengthen the child protection network.

Although the Ministries of Employment, Social Affairs, and Professional Training; Justice; Promotion of Women, Family, and Child Protection; and Education were responsible for combating child abuse, they were ineffective due to lack of coordination between the ministries and inadequate resources. In 2015 the Ministry of Education released a document in which it committed to protecting children in schools against abuses and to contributing to preventing, identifying, and reporting cases of children abused outside of schools. As of October, however, no reports of any action taken by the ministry were available.

Early and Forced Marriage: The law prohibits the marriage of men under age 20 and women under age 18 without parental consent. The law specifically penalizes anyone who forces a minor under age 18 to enter a religious or customary matrimonial union. Nevertheless, traditional marriages were performed with girls as young as 14 years old. The United Nations documented several cases of forced marriage and attempted forced marriage during the year.

According to the 2011-12 Demographic and Health Survey, the most recent survey available, 10 percent of women ages 20 to 24 were married before age 15, and 33 percent of women ages 20 to 24 were married before age 18.

In March authorities sentenced a man in Dabou Region to six months in prison for having sexual contact with a girl younger than age 15.

Female Genital Mutilation/Cutting (FGM/C): Information is provided in women's subsection above.

Sexual Exploitation of Children: The minimum age of consensual sex is 18. The law prohibits the use, recruitment, or offering of children for prostitution or pornographic films, pictures, or events. Violators can receive prison sentences ranging from five to 20 years and fines of five to 50 million CFA francs ($8,510 to $85,180). Statutory rape of a minor carries a punishment, if convicted, of one to three years in prison and a fine of 360,000 to one million CFA francs ($610 to $1,700).

The country was a source, transit, and destination country for children subjected to trafficking in persons, including sex trafficking. During the year the antitrafficking unit of the national police made several arrests of suspected child-sex traffickers.

In January authorities sentenced two individuals to six months in prison and a fine of two million CFA francs ($3,400) for pimping children, although the minimum sentence for coercing children into or offering them for prostitution is five years' imprisonment. Nine girls were exploited in prostitution in the restaurant owned by one of the perpetrators.

Also see the Department of State's *Trafficking in Persons Report* at www.state.gov/j/tip/rls/tiprpt/.

Displaced Children: Local NGOs reported thousands of children countrywide living on the streets. NGOs dedicated to helping these children found it difficult to estimate the extent of the problem or to determine whether these children had access to government services. No known government program specifically addressed the problem of children living on the streets.

In January the government launched a new service for the protection of children in conflict with the law. The inauguration of the Service for Judicial Protection for Children and Youth within the first instance tribunals took place in four districts-- two in Abidjan, one in Man, and one in Bouake. This service was established to help magistrates in charge of cases involving children find ways to reintegrate the children into society.

<u>International Child Abductions</u>: The country is not a party to the 1980 Hague Convention on the Civil Aspects of International Child Abduction. See the Department of State's *Annual Report on International Parental Child Abduction* at travel.state.gov/content/childabduction/en/legal/compliance.html.

Anti-Semitism

The country's Jewish community numbered fewer than 100 persons. There were no reports of anti-Semitic acts.

Trafficking in Persons

See the Department of State's *Trafficking in Persons Report* at www.state.gov/j/tip/rls/tiprpt/.

Persons with Disabilities

The law requires the government to educate and train persons with physical, mental, visual, auditory, and cerebral motor disabilities; hire them or help them find jobs; design houses and public facilities for wheelchair access; and adapt machines, tools, and work spaces for access and use by persons with disabilities as well as to provide them access to the judicial system. Wheelchair-accessible facilities were not common, however, and only five of the 36 tribunals were accessible by wheelchair. There were few training and job assistance programs for persons with disabilities. The law prohibits acts of violence against persons with disabilities and the abandonment of such persons, but there were no reports the government enforced these laws.

Persons with disabilities reportedly encountered serious discrimination in employment and education. While the government reserved 800 civil service jobs for persons with disabilities, government employers sometimes refused to employ such persons. Prisons and detention centers provided no accommodations for persons with disabilities.

The government financially supported special schools, training programs, associations, and artisans' cooperatives for persons with disabilities, but many persons with disabilities begged on urban streets and in commercial zones for lack of other economic opportunities. Although public schools did not bar persons with disabilities from attending, such schools lacked the resources to accommodate students with disabilities. Persons with mental disabilities often lived on the street.

The Ministry of Employment, Social Affairs, and Professional Training and the Federation of the Handicapped are responsible for protecting the rights of persons with disabilities.

In January the Ministry of Labor, Social Affairs, and Professional Training signed an agreement with La Libellule, a private jobs agency, to promote employment for persons with disabilities and to improve their social conditions. In June the ministry signed a similar agreement with six private enterprises.

National/Racial/Ethnic Minorities

The country has more than 60 ethnic groups, and ethnic discrimination was a problem. Authorities considered approximately 25 percent of the population foreign, although many within this category were second- or third-generation residents. Disputes among ethnic groups, often related to land, resulted in sporadic violence, particularly in the western region. Despite a 2013 procedural update that allows putative owners of land an additional 10 years to establish title, land ownership laws remained unclear and unimplemented, resulting in conflicts between native populations and other groups.

Although the law prohibits xenophobia, racism, and tribalism and makes these forms of intolerance punishable by five to 10 years' imprisonment, no prosecutions occurred during the year. There were instances in which police abused and harassed non-Ivoirian Africans residing in the country. Harassment by officials reflected the common belief that foreigners were responsible for high crime rates and identity card fraud.

Numerous persons were killed during the March intercommunal conflict between Loni farmers and Fulani herders, many of whom were Burkinabe, in Bouna, in the northeast. Dozos killed at least 27 persons during the conflict. An estimated 1,000 persons fled to Burkina Faso following the conflict. Authorities arrested the regional chief of the Dozos, who remained in detention awaiting trial at year's end.

Acts of Violence, Discrimination, and Other Abuses Based on Sexual Orientation and Gender Identity

The law's only mention of same-sex sexual activity is as a form of public indecency that carries a penalty of up to two years' imprisonment, the same prescribed for heterosexual acts performed in public. Antidiscrimination laws exist, but they do not address discrimination based on sexual orientation or gender identity (see section 7.d.).

Societal discrimination and violence against the LGBTI community were problems. In June, for example, LGBTI members gathered at an embassy to sign a condolence book following a terrorist attack on an LGBTI community abroad. Following the posting of a photograph of the signing on social media, residents assaulted LGBTI individuals pictured in the posting, and many subsequently fled their homes.

Law enforcement authorities were at times slow and ineffective in their response to societal violence targeting the LGBTI community. The few LGBTI organizations in the country operated freely but with caution.

HIV and AIDS Social Stigma

There was no official discrimination based on HIV/AIDS status. A 2014 law expressly condemns all forms of discrimination against persons with HIV and provides for their access to care and treatment. The law also prescribes fines for refusal of care or discrimination based on HIV/AIDS status.

The Ministry of Health and Public Hygiene managed a program to assist vulnerable populations (gay men, sex workers, and migrants) at high risk of acquiring HIV/AIDS. The Ministry for the Promotion of Women, Family, and Child Protection oversaw a program that directed food, education, and protection to orphans and vulnerable children, including those affected by HIV/AIDS.

In the most recent Demographic and Health Survey, approximately 47 percent of women and 45 percent of men in 2011-12 reported holding discriminatory attitudes towards those with HIV/AIDS. According to Afrobarometer's 2014-15 report, 76 percent of the population was tolerant of persons living with HIV/AIDS. Outside of hospitals and clinics, societal stigmatization was widespread, with the most overt discrimination directed at gay men with HIV/AIDS. Many persons with HIV/AIDS chose not to reveal their status to friends and family for fear of stigmatization.

Section 7. Worker Rights

a. Freedom of Association and the Right to Collective Bargaining

The law, including related regulations and statutory instruments, provides for the right of workers, except members of police and military services, to form or join unions of their choice, provides for the right to conduct legal strikes and bargain collectively, and prohibits antiunion discrimination by employers or others against union members or organizers. The law prohibits firing workers for union activities and provides for the reinstatement of dismissed workers within eight days of receiving a wrongful dismissal claim. The law allows unions in the formal sector to conduct their activities without interference. Worker organizations were independent of the government and political parties. Nevertheless, according to the International Trade Union Confederation, the law does not have any objective criteria to establish recognition of representative trade unions, which could allow public and private employers to refuse to negotiate with unions on the grounds they were not representative. Foreigners are required to obtain residency status, which takes three years, before they may hold union office.

The law requires a protracted series of negotiations and a six-day notification period before a strike may take place, making legal strikes difficult to organize and maintain. Workers must maintain a minimum coverage in services whose interruption may endanger the lives, security, or health of persons; create a national crisis that threatens the lives of the population; or affect the operation of equipment. Additionally, if authorities deem a strike to be a threat to public order, the president has broad powers to compel strikers to return to work under threat of sanctions. The president also may require that strikes in essential services go to arbitration, although the law does not describe what constitutes essential services.

Apart from large industrial farms and some trades, legal protections excluded most laborers in the informal sector, including small farms, roadside street stalls, and urban workshops.

Inadequate resources and inspections impeded the government's efforts to enforce applicable laws in the formal sector. Penalties for violations--fines between 10,000 and 100,000 CFA francs ($17 to $170)--were insufficient to deter violations. Administrative judicial procedures were subject to lengthy delays and appeals.

Before collective bargaining can begin, a union must represent 30 percent of workers. Collective bargaining agreements apply to employees in the formal sector, and many major businesses and civil-service sectors had them. Although the labor code may allow employers to refuse to negotiate, the Ministry of Employment, Social Affairs, and Professional Training did not receive any such complaints from unions. A well-known international trade union, however, reported that the government failed to remit union dues to several trade unions despite a valid collective bargaining agreement.

University and primary school teachers went on strike throughout the year. There were no reports of strikebreaking during the year.

The Ministry of Employment, Social Affairs, and Professional Training did not report any complaints of antiunion discrimination or employer interference in union functions during the year; however, the International Trade Union Confederation reported four cases in 2015. These cases included the arrest of a union representative for complaints about low wages, the military's occupation for several years of a union office, the forced dispersal of 200 strikers from the Ministry of Trade, and government violations of the right to strike by transferring union representatives and leaders to different parts of the country.

b. Prohibition of Forced or Compulsory Labor

The constitution and law prohibit all forms of forced or compulsory labor, including by children. Labor inspectors from the National School of Administration benefited from new modules on fighting against child labor as part of their training. Nevertheless, 739 inspections during the year did not result in any investigations into child labor crimes although the practice of child labor is widespread. A cooperation agreement between the governments of Cote d'Ivoire and Ghana to combat cross-border trafficking and child labor provides prison terms of one to five years for violators. It also specifies fines of between 500,000 to one million CFA francs ($850 to $1,700) if the offender is related to the child, a guardian, or a person in charge of the child's education who allows the child to perform hazardous work. Unrelated offenders face a 10- to 20-year prison term and a fine of five million to 20 million CFA francs ($8,510 to $34,070)--if they are convicted of involvement with forced child labor. Resources, inspections, penalties, and remediation were inadequate and insufficient to deter violations.

The National Monitoring Committee on Actions to Fight Trafficking, Exploitation, and Child Labor (NMC), chaired by First Lady Dominique Ouattara, and the Interministerial Committee are responsible for assessing government and donor actions on child labor. In 2015 the government drafted and completed the 2016-20 national action plan for the fight against trafficking in persons.

Forced and compulsory labor continued to occur in small-scale and commercial production of agricultural products, particularly on cocoa, coffee, pineapple, and rubber plantations, and in the informal labor sector, such as domestic work, nonindustrial farm labor, artisanal mines, street shops, and restaurants. Forced labor on cocoa, coffee, and pineapple plantations was limited to children (see section 7.c.). Reports of forced adult labor in rubber production primarily involved long hours and low pay for workers, who lived in conditions of effective indenture.

Also see the Department of State's *Trafficking in Persons Report* at www.state.gov/j/tip/rls/tiprpt/.

c. Prohibition of Child Labor and Minimum Age for Employment

The 2015 labor code raised the minimum age from 14 to 16 years old, although the minimum age for apprenticeships (14 years old) and hazardous work (18 years old) remained the same; minors under age 18 years old may not work at night. Although the law prohibits the exploitation of children in the workplace, the Ministry of Employment, Social Affairs, and Professional Training enforced the law effectively only in the civil service and large multinational companies.

The law prohibits child trafficking and the worst forms of child labor. Although lack of resources and inadequate training continued to hinder enforcement of child labor laws, the government took active steps to address the worst forms of child labor. The government worked on implementing its 2015-17 National Action Plan against Trafficking, Exploitation, and Child Labor and strengthened its national child labor monitoring system. In 2015 a targeted raid of various enterprises in the San Pedro area led to the rescue of 48 child victims of trafficking and the worst forms of child labor. As a result 22 persons were referred to the courts on trafficking-related charges. Beginning in 2014 the government implemented stricter regulations on the travel of minors to and from the country, requiring children and parents to provide documentation of family ties, including at least a birth certificate; however, these regulations were not always enforced.

The Department of the Fight against Child Labor within the Ministry of Employment, Social Affairs, and Professional Training, the NMC, and the Interministerial Committee led enforcement efforts. The 2015-17 National Action Plan had a budget of 9.6 billion CFA francs ($16.4 million). The plan calls for efforts to improve access to education, health care, and income-generating activities for children, as well as nationwide surveys, awareness campaigns, and other projects with local NGOs to highlight the dangers associated with child labor. First Lady Ouattara made the elimination of child labor a centerpiece of her efforts and continued to be actively involved.

The government engaged in partnerships with the International Labor Organization (ILO) to reduce child labor on cocoa farms. Through its International Program to Eliminate Child Labor, the ILO had two projects targeting child labor, both of which concluded in 2015.

The government worked with a foreign government entity on two child labor projects. The first project, implemented by the International Cocoa Initiative, was the recently inaugurated Eliminating Child Labor in Cocoa project. The goal of the four-year, 2.6 billion CFA francs ($4.5 million) project was to assist the country's 50 cocoa growing communities to develop and implement community action plans and to provide direct education and livelihood services to reduce the use of child labor in the cocoa sector. The second project was the third and final survey to measure the prevalence of child labor in cocoa growing areas in the country and in Ghana, pursuant to the declaration and accompanying framework to support the implementation of the Harkin-Engel Protocol. The survey was scheduled for the 2018-19 cocoa growing season as a follow up to earlier surveys in 2008-09 and 2013-14.

The government coordinated with NGOs to conduct campaigns to sensitize farm families about child labor, based on the government's list of prohibited worst forms of child labor. Consequently, local domestic worker organizations sought to prevent the exploitation of children in domestic work. Other NGOs campaigned against child trafficking, child labor, and the sexual abuse of children.

The punishment for violating the law includes a prison term of one to five years and a fine of 500,000 to one million CFA francs ($850 to $1,700). The penalties were not sufficient to deter violations, and the government did not effectively enforce the law. Child labor remained a widespread problem, particularly on cocoa and coffee plantations and in gold and diamond mines.

Children routinely worked on family farms or as vendors, shoe shiners, errand boys, domestic helpers, street restaurant vendors, and car watchers and washers. Some girls as young as nine years old reportedly worked as domestic servants, often within their extended family networks. While the overall prevalence of child labor decreased, children in rural areas continued to work on cocoa farms under hazardous conditions, including risk of injury from machetes, physical strain from carrying heavy loads, and exposure to harmful chemicals. A small percentage of the children working on cocoa farms had no family ties to the farmers, but most worked on family farms or with their parents. According to a 2014 ILO report, approximately 40 percent of children between ages five and 14 worked, and nearly a quarter of all children combined work and school.

Also see the Department of Labor's *Findings on the Worst Forms of Child Labor* at www.dol.gov/ilab/reports/child-labor/findings/.

d. Discrimination with Respect to Employment and Occupation

The law prohibits employment and occupation discrimination based on sex, age, national origin, citizenship, race, religion, political opinion, and social origin, but the law does not address discrimination based on sexual orientation and/or gender identity, color, or language. A 2014 law specifically prohibits workplace discrimination based on HIV/AIDS status, but does not address other communicable diseases. The labor code passed in July 2015 includes provisions to promote access to employment for persons with disabilities. It stipulates that employers must reserve a quota of jobs for qualified handicapped applicants. The law does not provide for penalties for employment discrimination.

The government did not always effectively enforce the law. Discrimination in employment and occupation occurred with respect to gender, nationality, persons with disabilities, and LGBTI persons (see section 6). While women in the formal sector received the same pay and paid the same taxes as men, some employers resisted hiring women.

While the law provides the same protections for migrant workers in the formal sector as it does for citizens, most faced discrimination in terms of wages and treatment.

e. Acceptable Conditions of Work

The minimum wage for all professions other than the agricultural sector was 60,000 CFA francs per month ($100). The agricultural minimum wage was 25,000 CFA francs ($40) per month. The official estimate for the poverty income level was between 500 and 700 CFA francs ($0.85 and $1.19) per day. The Ministry of Employment, Social Affairs, and Professional Training is responsible for enforcing the minimum wage. The government enforced the law only for salaried workers employed by the government or registered with the social security office. Labor unions contributed to effective implementation of the minimum salary requirements in the formal sector. Labor federations attempted to fight for just treatment under the law for workers when companies failed to meet minimum salary requirements or discriminated between classes of workers, such as women or local versus foreign workers.

The law does not stipulate equal pay for equal work. There were no reports the government took action to rectify the large salary discrepancies between foreign non-African employees and their African colleagues employed by the same companies.

The standard legal workweek is 40 hours. The law requires overtime pay for additional hours and provides for at least one 24-hour rest period per week. The law does not prohibit compulsory overtime.

The law establishes occupational safety and health standards in the formal sector. The law provides for the establishment of a committee of occupational, safety, and health representatives responsible for verifying protection and worker health at workplaces. Such committees are to be composed of union members. The chair of the committee could report unhealthy and unsafe working conditions to the labor inspector without penalty. The law does not cover several million foreign migrant workers or workers in the informal sector, who accounted for 70 percent of the nonagricultural economy. The government did not effectively enforce the law and penalties were insufficient to deter violations (500,000 to one million CFA francs ($850 to $1,700).

By law workers in the formal sector have the right to remove themselves from situations that endanger their health or safety without jeopardy to their employment. They may utilize the inspection system of the Ministry of Employment, Social Affairs, and Professional Training to document dangerous working conditions. Authorities effectively protected employees in this situation.

The Ministry of Employment, Social Affairs, and Professional Training estimated the number of labor inspectors at no more than 300, insufficient to enforce the law effectively. Labor inspectors reportedly accepted bribes to ignore violations.

While the law requires businesses to provide medical services for their employees, small firms, businesses in the informal sector, households employing domestic staff, and farms (particularly during the seasonal harvests) did not comply. Excessive hours of work were common, and employers rarely recorded and seldom paid overtime hours in accordance with the law. In particular, employees in the informal manufacturing sector often worked without adequate protective gear.

Enforcement of provision of medical services in the informal sector, generally, was nonexistent.